She
Persisted

. . . .

FLORENCE NIGHTINGALE

. . . .

— INSPIRED BY —

She Persisted

by Chelsea Clinton & Alexandra Boiger

· ·

FLORENCE NIGHTINGALE

· ·

Written by
Shelli R. Johannes

Interior illustrations by
Gillian Flint

PHILOMEL

⌒ *To* ⌒

*all the first responders, nurses, doctors, and
caretakers who sacrificed everything to work on the front
lines of the pandemic and save countless lives. You are true
heroes, and Florence Nightingale would be proud!*

PHILOMEL BOOKS
An imprint of Penguin Random House LLC, New York

First published in the United States of America by Philomel Books,
an imprint of Penguin Random House LLC, 2023

Text copyright © 2023 by Chelsea Clinton
Illustrations copyright © 2023 by Alexandra Boiger

Philomel Books is a registered trademark of Penguin Random House LLC.

Visit us online at penguinrandomhouse.com.

Library of Congress Cataloging-in-Publication Data is available.

Printed in the United States of America

HC ISBN 9780593529003
10 9 8 7 6 5 4 3 2 1

PB ISBN 9780593529010
10 9 8 7 6 5 4 3 2 1

WOR

Edited by Talia Benamy and Jill Santopolo.
Design by Ellice M. Lee.
Text set in LTC Kennerley Pro.

Dear Reader,

As Sally Ride and Marian Wright Edelman both powerfully said, "You can't be what you can't see." When Sally said that, she meant that it was hard to dream of being an astronaut, like she was, or a doctor or an athlete or anything at all if you didn't see someone like you who already had lived that dream. She especially was talking about seeing women in jobs that historically were held by men.

I wrote the first *She Persisted* and the books that came after it because I wanted young girls—and children of all genders—to see women who worked hard to live their dreams. And I wanted all of us to see examples of persistence in the face of different challenges to help inspire us in our own lives.

I'm so thrilled now to partner with a sisterhood of writers to bring longer, more in-depth versions of these stories of women's persistence and achievement to readers. I hope you enjoy these chapter books as much as I do and find them inspiring and empowering.

And remember: If anyone ever tells you no, if anyone ever says your voice isn't important or your dreams are too big, remember these women. They persisted and so should you.

Warmly,
Chelsea Clinton

She Persisted

....

FLORENCE NIGHTINGALE

TABLE OF CONTENTS

....

································

The Girl Who Loved Math

Florence Nightingale never wanted to be a proper lady!

While some girls enjoyed sewing, Florence loved math. But that was just the beginning. Florence became a pioneer in nursing and is one of the most famous nurses of all time. She developed many of the hygiene procedures we use today, such as washing hands, wearing masks, and keeping hospitals clean.

But for all she would do in her life, Florence's road to becoming a nurse wasn't easy.

Florence Nightingale was born in Florence, Italy, on May 12, 1820. Her sister, Parthenope, was only a year old at the time. Their English parents, William and Frances (also known as Fanny), were on a three-year honeymoon around Europe when the girls were born. Because the Nightingales loved Italy so much, they named the girls after Italian cities.

Florence and Parthenope (or "Pop," as Florence called her) lived a very privileged life. William was a wealthy banker and politician. And Frances was a true socialite. She loved throwing fancy parties and inviting those she considered to be the brightest minds of the time. They also had many visits from family and friends. No matter who showed up, Frances encouraged her daughters to mingle with their company.

But Florence was not interested in parties. She felt awkward and didn't like being the center of attention. Florence would often butt heads with her mother, especially when Fanny pushed her daughters to lead what she considered a normal life for white, wealthy English women in the 1800s.

The Nightingales lived in two different houses throughout the year. The houses were so big they even had their own names! In the winter, the Nightingales lived in their estate at Embley Park, located south of London. The mansion had many bedrooms and sat on five square miles of beautiful countryside. In the summer, the family moved north to their country home, Lea Hurst.

Florence (nicknamed Flo) loved her time at Lea Hurst. The house sat at the edge of a beautiful village overlooking rolling hills and sloping green meadows. She enjoyed wandering through the gardens and reading.

While Pop was interested in music, art, and sewing, Florence showed a love for math and science. She collected shells and coins and then spent hours arranging them based on their colors, sizes, and shapes. Once they were organized, Florence would make notes about them in tables and lists. In fact, Florence wrote her first letter in 1826, when she was six years old, and in it, she categorized and counted all the animals she saw at the nearby zoo.

Math was a special talent Florence used throughout her life.

When Florence was young, most girls were
not allowed to attend school or receive an education! But Florence's father knew his daughters
were smart, so he educated them himself at home.

Flo and Pop would visit their dad's office

every day to learn different subjects. Florence would rise early and focus on her lessons from the day before. William taught his daughters other languages, English grammar, philosophy, and history. He also brought in tutors and governesses to teach other subjects, like botany (the study of plants), geography, drawing, and piano. Florence was a bookworm and a great student who could speak, read, and write in French, German, Italian, Greek, and Latin.

William loved math, just like his daughter, and eventually taught Florence arithmetic, geometry, and algebra. However, Fanny did not approve of all the time the girls spent learning. Fanny wanted Flo and Pop to focus on marrying wealthy men who would care for them. In those days, working and earning money was considered a man's role in wealthier families. This view of women made Florence angry. She didn't like the social norms that were expected of women. While she argued with her mother often, Flo was very close to her father. They spent hours discussing and debating philosophy. He introduced Florence to scientists and mathematicians who visited their home, including Adolphe Quetelet, who is considered one of the founders of statistics (the science of collecting, organizing, and analyzing numbers). Florence loved intellectual conversations and easily impressed adults with all her knowledge.

As she grew older, Florence's home education stopped. Her life became filled with social events and parties. But she wasn't happy with this lifestyle, later writing, "Why have women passion,

intellect, and moral activity—these three—and a place in society where no one of the three can be exercised?"

Her relationship with Fanny wasn't easy, and the same was true of her relationship with her sister, Pop. Flo wondered how she could be in the same family yet be so different! Pop loved the life of a Victorian woman and spent her time with Fanny in the drawing room, polishing silverware and setting a proper table.

Even though Florence wanted her mother's approval, she knew that life was not for her.

Flo wanted something more.

·····························

A Call to Nursing

As a teenager, Florence silently questioned her purpose in life.

One day when she was about seventeen, Flo decided to walk in the garden and read under her favorite tree. There, she experienced what she later referred to as a call to service from God. This vision sparked Florence's deep passion for nursing, but it wasn't the only thing that did. Her whole life seemed to point her in that direction.

When she was young, instead of playing with other kids, Florence often joined her mother on trips to the local village. She would ride her horse and deliver food to sick and hungry neighbors.

During the 1837 flu epidemic, around the same time as her call to service, Florence was the only one in her household who didn't get sick. She nursed her friends and family back to health, sitting with them for hours and taking notes on their symptoms. But her need to help others didn't end there. When she wasn't taking care of people, she loved taking care of animals.

One day, Florence heard that her neighbor's sheepdog, Cap, had injured his leg. Unfortunately, the owner couldn't pay an expert to fix the leg. So Florence offered to take care of Cap herself. She sat with Cap and put warm compresses that she

made from old flannel on the wound. Eventually, she nursed Cap back to health so he could lead a long and happy life. Some say that Cap was one of Florence's first patients.

Florence had many pets of her own during her lifetime, including more than sixty cats, a cicada named Plato, an owl named Athena, Peggie the pony, several dogs named Peppercorn, Teazer, and Captain, a parrot, two chameleons, and two tortoises named Mr. and Mrs. Hill.

In late 1837, not long after Florence's vision in the garden, the Nightingales decided to take both of their daughters on an extended tour of Europe. This was common for upper-class British people during the time period, and it was designed to educate girls about the world and teach them how to be what society considered a proper lady. Florence spent much of the trip recording notes on population statistics and hospital data.

The family attended operas in Italy and parties in Paris. At one of these parties, Florence met a salon hostess named Mary Clarke who believed that women were equal to men. She taught Florence that there were many opportunities open to educated women. Mary made a big impression on Flo. Even though there was quite an age difference, the two remained close for many years.

When the family returned to England, Fanny continued to pressure her girls to be proper Victorian ladies and to think about marrying wealthy men. But Florence didn't want to be a lady in the way that was expected of her in society, and she certainly didn't want to get married!

She didn't want anything or anyone to get in the way of her nursing dreams.

When Florence reached her early twenties, she finally got up the nerve to tell her parents that she wanted to be a nurse. Fanny was shocked at the idea, and both parents forbade Florence from even considering the career. In those days, many people feared hospitals because sometimes people left in worse conditions than when they arrived.

Plus, many people thought nurses were rude, untrained, unskilled, and from a lower class.

But Florence didn't agree! She secretly continued wondering how she could follow her dream.

For the next couple of years, Florence was frustrated that she could not seek out her true purpose. She turned down many marriage proposals and looked for ways to study nursing by taking care of friends, neighbors, and family members. She even begged her parents to let her train at the local Salisbury Infirmary.

But they would not budge on their decision.

Instead, William and Fanny sent Flo off to Europe with their friends, hoping she would forget all about nursing. But Florence was determined to follow her heart and her calling. Even as she traveled across Europe, Florence secretly educated herself. She sneaked in visits to hospitals and convents. She met with nuns and took notes on how they cared for their patients, hoping to understand God's call to service.

In 1848, Florence visited Rome and befriended a married couple, Sidney and Elizabeth Herbert. Sidney was an important member of the British government, and he would eventually play a huge role in Florence's life.

For the next several years, Florence traveled across Greece and Egypt. Wherever she went, Florence tried to learn how she could help people and animals. In Greece, she rescued a baby owl and named her Athena. Flo carried the pet owl on her shoulder and in her pocket. She eventually brought Athena back to England and loved the owl deeply until its death.

All of these traveling experiences turned out to be good for Florence. Not only did she learn more about the different ways she could help people, but Flo also met friends who became significant people in her life. Years later, Sidney would call on Florence to fill a crucial role.

But for now, she continued to dream of nursing.

Against All Odds

Florence remained determined to pursue her dream of becoming a nurse.

When she finally returned to England in 1850, she made a big decision! Against her family's wishes, Flo enrolled as a nursing student at the Deaconesses Institute in Kaiserswerth, Germany. The institute helped the poor and cared for women who had been imprisoned and children who were homeless. Florence treated sick people, gave out medicine, and helped with minor operations.

By 1851, the institute had grown into a famous training school for woman teachers and nurses. Florence learned more about basic nursing skills, the importance of observing patients, and good hospital organization.

Flo was finally in her element, writing, "Now I know what it is to love life!"

But Florence didn't stop there. After her training, she continued visiting and inspecting hospitals throughout Paris, London, Edinburgh, and Dublin.

In 1853, Florence was offered her first professional job as the superintendent at London's Establishment of Gentlewomen during Illness that was located in a private home. This place was for women who did not have proper health care.

Florence was asked to be in charge. Of course, she happily said yes.

By this time, her family had reluctantly accepted her passion for nursing. Flo's father even gave her an extra five hundred pounds a year (which is about $83,000 today!). This money helped Florence continue to pursue her nursing career.

For the next year, Florence used her skills to make big changes as superintendent. She improved training for nurses, made sure there was hot water on every floor, and built a lift to carry up meals to patients. She wrote reports, letters, and lists to document information on sickness, health, and healing. She called these ideas the "art and science of nursing." When a devastating disease called cholera started to spread in the area, Florence also volunteered at Middlesex Hospital to help

take care of the many sick patients.

Florence was becoming known for her suc-cess in nursing. And eventually, all her hard work, training, and passion paid off.

In October 1853, the Crimean War started between Russia and Turkey. Britain and France joined in the fight. But even though the war was fought in Russia, the British military hospitals were located in Scutari, Turkey.

A British newspaper began publishing articles about British soldiers living in hospitals with horrible conditions. The stories reported that the men were not dying in battle. Instead, they were dying of sickness, infections, and a lack of healthy food. When people read about this, they were furious!

In response, Florence's old friend Sidney Herbert, who was the British Secretary of State for War, asked Florence to go to the military hospital in Scutari and help straighten things out. He even gave her an official title: the Superintendent of the Female Nursing Establishment of the English General Hospitals in Turkey.

Florence was excited to use her passion and nursing skills for the war effort. Sidney gave Florence permission to organize a group of woman nurses. She had less than a week to gather supplies, recruit nurses, and prepare for the trip.

Florence jumped into action!

Many nurses tried to volunteer at the War Office, including Mary Seacole, a British Jamaican nurse who also became famous for helping wounded soldiers on the Crimean battlefront.

Florence eventually chose thirty-eight women to travel with her from England to Turkey. Flo packed a chest filled with medicines to treat malaria and fevers. The box also contained a small set of scales and glass beakers to measure liquids correctly.

Soon Florence was ready to leave. She didn't know that this role would change her life forever and make her one of the most famous nurses in history.

....

Lady with the Lamp

On October 21, 1854, Florence and her nurses left for Turkey.

The journey was long and hard. Over the next thirteen days, they went from England to France and then across the Mediterranean Sea. They traveled part of the way by horse and carriage, but most of the trip was spent on an old boat called *Vectis*. The traveling conditions were horrible. They lived with cockroaches on board and faced stormy weather and rough waters. Florence spent most of the trip battling terrible seasickness.

Finally, on November 3, they arrived in Scutari. But even though Sidney had sent them, Florence and her nurses were not welcomed by the male British officers and doctors. Flo had been granted permissions that no woman had ever had in the army's history, and the men weren't happy about it. But she insisted on helping anyway. Florence and her nurses were given a tiny kitchen and a few small bedrooms that had holes in the walls and leaky roofs. Determined to make it work, they settled in and visited the soldiers.

They were shocked and horrified at what they saw.

The hospital was overcrowded, with over

two thousand sick, injured, and dying soldiers and only a handful of doctors to help. The facilities were filthy. There were rats and fleas everywhere. The soldiers were in grimy clothes and lying in dirt, blood, and poop from broken toilets. The food was moldy and full of maggots. They had no sheets or towels, operating tables, or proper medical supplies. Florence immediately asked for towels and soap to begin cleaning up. She insisted the nurses wash all the linens and clothes and scrub the floors. But without the right supplies, they could only do so much!

Within days, thousands more injured soldiers began arriving from battle. The soldiers had infectious diseases, the hospital became even more overcrowded, and the unclean conditions got worse with so many people coming in. The hospital also had bad airflow, so germs stayed in the air and got more people sick. The sewer system was broken, which meant things got filthy quickly. The nurses ran out of basic supplies such as beds, linens, bandages, and soap—everything they needed to keep the hospital clean and their patients safe and healthy.

The horrible conditions were unbearable for the sick and injured soldiers, and many of them died.

Florence was devastated and felt helpless, but she persisted and tried to help wherever she could. She later wrote about the sick soldiers, "While I live, I fight their cause."

That's when Florence's love of math came in handy. At the time, no one was tracking the deaths. In between taking care of soldiers and trying to improve hospital conditions, Florence began recording and studying their causes of death. She quickly noticed that soldiers were dying from preventable diseases such as typhus, typhoid, cholera, and dysentery. Many soldiers were also dying from bad cases of frostbite and gangrene, things that were easily treated but that had been ignored.

When Florence did the math, she discovered that soldiers were ten times more likely to die from disease than battle wounds. She showed that if she could make the hospital cleaner, she could significantly reduce the number of deaths. These numbers gave her hope.

Florence collected her data and sent many letters to Sidney and Queen Victoria, explaining her findings and begging for help. Her letters grabbed the attention of government officials, newspapers, and donors who sent over a few necessities. She even inspired the queen to send extra supplies and fresh food.

Even with these extra measures, during that first winter, more than four thousand soldiers died.

Eventually, Florence realized something very important. The only way she could make the difference she wanted and save every life she could was to change the entire system of care! She immediately got to work and made a plan. Florence and the hospital staff brought in more clean water and nutritious food. They removed the trash and sanitized everything to keep the germs and bacteria away. Florence also made sure soldiers had clean laundry and clean clothes.

Florence also noticed a strong connection between the soldiers' mental and physical health.

After seeing that, she made sure all the soldiers received personal and special care. She started the nurse call system, which we still use a version of today in our hospitals. The soldiers used bells to call for a nurse whenever they needed help. Florence also created a special area for recovering soldiers that provided a classroom and a library to help them pass the time.

In addition to completing her regular duties and writing reports, Florence walked through the four-mile-long hospital every night. She carried an oil lamp along the dark and damp halls, wearing a black dress over her nurse's uniform. Flo checked on the wounded soldiers. She replaced soiled bandages, bathed dirty patients, and helped them write letters to their families back home. This special care helped the men and saved more lives.

soon widely reported in the press.

To honor Florence's work, Queen Victoria awarded her with a gold brooch (a type of pin) that was decorated with a red Saint George's cross, three stars, and diamonds. The inscription on the front read "Blessed are the Merciful." The Queen also inscribed a personal message: "To Miss Florence Nightingale, as a mark of esteem and gratitude for her devotion towards the Queen's brave soldiers."

Florence and her nurses worked hard and saved many lives!

But Flo was not always the one taking care of others. While she was in Turkey, Florence caught a severe illness called Crimean fever and became a patient herself. The disease left her with fevers, pain, and fatigue for the rest of her life.

After the war, because of her illness, Florence never actively practiced nursing again. However, she did not give up. She persisted in improving health care and continued her work for many years to come.

CHAPTER 5

A Heroine and a Pioneer

By the time the war was over, the military hospitals in Scutari were much more efficient, with fewer deaths than when Florence arrived.

Meanwhile, back in England, the legend of the Lady with the Lamp grew larger than life. Songs and poems were dedicated to Florence Nightingale. And the press continued reporting the soldiers' stories about her kindness and care.

Florence was a hero!

But she didn't care for fame or attention.

On her way back from Turkey, Florence used the name Miss Smith so she could quietly return to Lea Hurst. But the effects of her illness kept her mostly bedridden for the rest of her life. Even though the war was over, Flo still had a lot of regret and sadness about all the lost lives in Scutari. She wrote: "The very first require ment in a hospital is that it should do the sick no harm." Now she was more determined than ever to improve health care in all hospitals.

Florence started doing that work from her bed. She prepared an eight-hundred-page report that discussed all her findings from working at Scutari Hospital during the Crimean War. This report helped Queen Victoria start the Royal Commission on the Health of the Army, which

led to changes across hospitals throughout Great Britain. In appreciation of Florence's hard work, a public fund was created in her honor called the Nightingale Fund. Citizens, soldiers, and former patients donated over $44,000, which is equal to about 7 million dollars today!

During this time, Florence was still very sick.

Luckily, she was wealthy enough to afford private health care in her home, but she knew that many British citizens did not have that option. To address this concern, Florence wrote and published two books on nursing: *Notes on Hospitals* and *Notes on Nursing*. These books included practical tips that families and caretakers could use with their sick loved ones. Florence explained the importance of washing hands, keeping everything clean, preparing foods properly, and disposing of garbage. This information helped people give their loved ones the best possible care.

In 1860, Florence used the Nightingale Fund

to start the Nightingale Home and Training School for Nurses. The school is still a part of King's College London today.

The school opened with a small group of students, and it was the first nonreligious institution to offer professional nurse training. Soon, women from the wealthy upper classes started enrolling at the school to follow in Flo's footsteps. From 1860 to 1900, about two thousand nurses completed the required training.

Despite being sick and confined to her bedroom, Florence kept making a difference! She spent years in bed writing and talking to people about proper nurse training and health care improvements.

Throughout her life, she wrote nineteen thousand letters and diary entries. These included information about many things: her work in nurs-ing, her dislike of fancy society, and the illness she struggled with until her death. In addition to her letters, she also wrote hundreds of reports, pamphlets, and books on various topics, including nursing, hospital organization, and the health care system.

Florence became an important figure in Britain and around the world, sharing her knowl-edge and resources with many countries. She gave advice on how to run military hospitals to kings and queens around the world. And during the Civil War, Florence advised the US about how to best manage field hospitals. Later, both sides of the Franco-Prussian War asked for Florence's advice.

Florence always helped because she believed everyone deserved proper care.

Over the years, Florence was recognized in many different ways. She helped support the foundation of the British Red Cross and became a member of the organization's Ladies' Committee. Queen Victoria gave her the Royal Red Cross for excellence in military nursing, and Florence

was the first of only eight women ever to accept the Order of Merit, Britain's highest honor for non-soldiers. Later, Florence became the second woman to receive the Freedom of the City of London for her outstanding achievements. This was the highest honor the city could award.

On August 13, 1910, Florence died in her London home at age ninety. She was buried at the family plot in Embley Park. Many nurses attended her memorial service.

But Florence's legacy never died.

....

CHAPTER 6

Florence's Legacy

Florence Nightingale changed the face of nursing forever!

She made a huge impact throughout her life by using math skills and her passion for helping people. She also encouraged women to be brave and follow their dreams, no matter what society told them to do. Her name and legacy have survived through the years in many ways.

After Florence's death, the International

Committee of the Red Cross created the Florence Nightingale Medal. This international award is given every two years to outstanding nurses for their courage and devotion to victims of a war or natural disaster, and for having a pioneering spirit in public health and nurse education. Every

year, International Nurses Day honors Florence's birthday on May 12, and celebrates nurses around the world for their hard work and dedication.

In 2010, the Florence Nightingale Museum reopened on Florence's birthday to honor the hundredth anniversary of her death. The London museum houses more than two thousand arti-facts, including her famous lamp, medicine chest, black dress, and nursing uniform.

Florence defied all odds for women during her time.

She became an incredibly successful nurse and transformed health care to help make it what it is today. Florence proved that hygiene, sani-tation, and good ventilation are critical. She also showed that proper lighting, healthy food, and personal care are equally important. Florence understood the need for social distancing and made sure spaces were spread out and well ventilated to keep germs from spreading. Her hospital designs, known as Nightingale wards, have changed how hospitals are designed today.

In addition to her nursing accomplishments, Florence is also remembered as a brilliant mathematician. She created "rose diagrams" in which she displayed numbers in colorful pictures that made them easy to read and understand. She

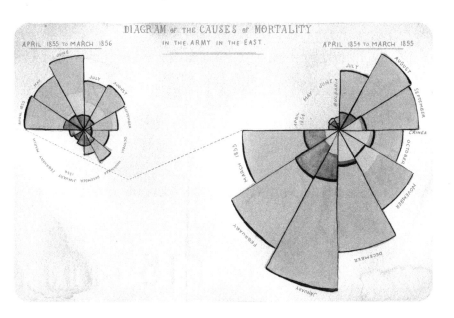

received several awards for her math skills. In fact, she was the first woman to be elected to the Royal Statistical Society in London. Her love for reasoning, questioning, calculating, and coming to conclusions made her a true mathematician at heart.

Florence is still an inspiration to nurses around the globe.

Today, nurses are recognized as essential, highly skilled health care professionals. During the COVID-19 pandemic, people around the world saw how hard nurses fought for their patients. And we used Florence's hygiene methods of washing hands, wearing masks, and staying six feet apart to keep one another safe.

Florence Nightingale started out as a headstrong girl with a very organized shell collection.

But in the end, she became a famous nurse and a well-respected mathematician. She spent her life fighting for a woman's right to study math and science and to be a nurse.

Florence was determined to succeed in nursing, no matter what anyone said. She persisted in showing the world that she, and other women, could do just that. As she once said, "You want to do the thing that is good, whether it is 'suitable for a woman' or not."

HOW YOU CAN PERSIST

by Shelli R. Johannes

To honor Florence Nightingale's persistence and trailblazing in health care and nursing, try some of these activities with your friends and family:

1. Find ways to volunteer in your local community. Search for local organizations where you and your

family can help the homeless, sick, or elderly. You can do arts and crafts, bake treats, create care packages, sort medical or school supplies, or participate in family volunteer days.

2. Talk to your doctor or nurse about health. On your next doctor visit, ask your doctor or nurse about their job and the important work they do every day. You can also ask questions about your own health and learn about the different ways you can stay healthy. Maybe your doctor or nurse can show you your patient profile and growth chart. See how much you've grown this year!

3. Offer to clean your home. Ask your

parents if you can help when they clean the house. For example, you can dust, vacuum, make your bed, or wash dishes. Every little thing adds up. Plus, you will get major bonus points!

4. Practice good hygiene in home and at school. Remember to wash your hands frequently to prevent germs. You could also have a soap-making party where you and your friends make colorful, sweet-smelling soaps to help everyone practice good handwashing.

5. Celebrate International Nurses Day on May 12. On this day, we celebrate Florence Nightingale's birthday as well as honor all nurses and their work in health care. Be sure to thank a nurse

for all their incredible work. You can send a letter, make a card, or post about it online.

6. Put together your own first aid kit. Grab a shoebox and decorate the outside. You and your family or friends can add in things like fun Band-Aids, scissors, gauze wrapping, ointment for cuts and bug bites, and any other items you might need.

7. Write a letter or a postcard, or write in a journal. Get a journal and record the things you do during the day. Or write a letter or postcard to a family or friend—just to say hello.

Acknowledgments

To Julie Stokes and Joey/Beth Bowers for lending me your beautiful homes when I desperately needed a place to write.

To Ursula and Jan for always keeping me balanced and believing that the universe has my back.

To my longtime BFFs Amy, Cat, and Beth for all the side-splitting laughs and the thirty-five years of friendship and unconditional love.

To the Country Lane Gals for honoring my introverted ways. Thank you for dragging me out of my writing cave so I don't forget to have fun!

To Katie Anderson, Sarah Frances Hardy, Jen Jabaley, and Kristin Tubb for helping me "persist" through the hard times, and for being first to celebrate the good ones.

To Zibby Owens and the "Moms Don't Have Time to Read Books" book club family for getting me through all those lonely days during the pandemic.

To Lara Perkins at ABLA for the last ten years of believing in me and for helping me make my dreams come true. I appreciate you!

To my amazing Philomel editors, Jill Santopolo and Talia Benamy, for giving me this opportunity to write about a true woman hero. I'm honored to be a part of the "Persisterhood" for life.

To all of my family, especially Dad, Gary, and Michelle, for loving me for my strengths, in spite of my flaws.

To Mom for being my #1 reader, coming to every signing, believing in me, and for all the things you've done for me and never got thanked enough . . . thank you!

To Kim Derting for being my partner in crime and for always having my back—no matter what. You are "my person."

To my two unicorns, Madelyn and Gray, for being funny, kind, smart, and just plain fun. You are amazing human beings, and I can't wait to see how you change the world. Be brave, be bold, be you!

To my husband and best friend, Ali, for loving me through twenty years of ups and downs and for all the amazing times in between. I could not have followed my passion without your undying support, advice, brainstorming, encouragement, and positivity. AM BYTH A THU HWANT.

To all of the kids, readers, bloggers, TikTokers, tweeters, educators, and families for your ongoing support and for taking the time to read my words.

To all the indie bookstores, especially Virginia Highland Books, Little Shop of Stories, and Brave and Kind Books, for always supporting me and my books.

To all the nurses and doctors and caretakers who put their lives on the line to help the sick during the COVID pandemic, you are true heroes.

To all human beings on this earth, we can do much better. Be kind.

And lastly, to Florence Nightingale and all the woman scientists who often get overlooked, I see you. Thank you for "persisting" and paving the way for girls and women to follow their dreams.

⤙ *References* ⤚

Alexander, Kerri Lee. "Florence Nightingale."
National Women's History Museum. 2019.
https://www.womenshistory.org/education
-resources/biographies/florence-nightingale.
Biography.com Editors. "Florence Nightingale."
The Biography.com website. A&E Networks
Television, last modified May 6, 2021. https://
www.biography.com/scientist/florence
-nightingale.
Bostridge, Mark. *Florence Nightingale: The
Making of an Icon.* New York: Farrar, Straus
and Giroux, 2008.
"Florence Nightingale Facts for Kids." *National*

Geographic Kids, June 2, 2020. https://www
.natgeokids.com/uk/discover/history/general
-history/florence-nightingale/.

Florence Nightingale Museum. "The Crimean War."
Florence Nightingale Museum. https://www
.florence-nightingale.co.uk/the-crimean-war/.

Florence Nightingale Museum. "Florence
Nightingale biography." Florence Nightingale
Museum. https://www.florence-nightingale
.co.uk/florence-nightingale-biography/.

Florence Nightingale Museum. "St Thomas'
Hospital." Florence Nightingale Museum.
https://www.florence-nightingale.co.uk
/st-thomas-hospital/.

Hammer, Joshua. "The Defiance of Florence
Nightingale." *Smithsonian Magazine,* March
2020. https://www.smithsonianmag.com

/history/the-worlds-most-famous-nurse
-florence-nightingale-180974155/.

Haynes, Suyin. "How Florence Nightingale
Paved the Way for the Heroic Work of Nurses
Today." *Time*, May 12, 2020. https://time.com
/5835150/florence-nightingale-legacy-nurses/.

History.com Editors. "Florence Nightingale."
History. A&E Television Networks, last modified March 8, 2022. https://www.history.com
/topics/womens-history/florence-nightingale-1.

Kennedy, Maev. "Florence Nightingale Letters
Brought Together Online." *The Guardian*,
August 20, 2014. https://www.theguardian
.com/culture/2014
/aug/20/florence-nightingale-letters-online.

The National Archives. "Florence Nightingale."
Education: Classroom Resources. The

National Archives, March 25, 2021.
https://www.nationalarchives.gov.uk
/education/resources/florence-nightingale/.

Rizzo, Johnna. "Florence Nightingale." Women
Heroes. *National Geographic Kids*, February
16, 2021. https://kids.nationalgeographic.com
/history/article/florence-nightingale.

Selanders, Louise. "Florence Nightingale—British
Nurse, Statistician, and Social Reformer."
Encyclopaedia Britannica, last modified May 8,
2022. https://www.britannica.com/biography
/Florence-Nightingale.

Sweet, Victoria. "Far More than a Lady with a
Lamp." *The New York Times*, March 3, 2014.
https://www.nytimes.com/2014/03/04
/health/florence-nightingales-wisdom.html.

SHELLI R. JOHANNES is the author of the Cece Loves Science series and the Theo TheSaurus picture books. A science and animal lover, she can often be found volunteering with animal conservation groups or rescuing strays off the side of the highway. Shelli lives in Atlanta with her husband, two kids, and a whole bunch of pets.

You can visit Shelli R. Johannes online at
SRJohannes.com
or follow her on Twitter and Instagram
@SRJohannes

GILLIAN FLINT has worked as a professional illustrator since earning an animation and illustration degree in 2003. Her work has since been published in the UK, USA and Australia. In her spare time, Gillian enjoys reading, spending time with her family and puttering about in the garden on sunny days. She lives in the northwest of England.

You can visit Gillian Flint online at
gillianflint.com
or follow her on Twitter
@GillianFlint
and on Instagram
@gillianflint_illustration

CHELSEA CLINTON is the author of the #1 *New York Times* bestseller *She Persisted: 13 American Women Who Changed the World*; *She Persisted Around the World: 13 Women Who Changed History*; *She Persisted in Sports: American Olympians Who Changed the Game*; *Don't Let Them Disappear: 12 Endangered Species Across the Globe*; *It's Your World: Get Informed, Get Inspired & Get Going!*; *Start Now!: You Can Make a Difference*; with Hillary Clinton, *Grandma's Gardens* and *Gutsy Women*; and, with Devi Sridhar, *Governing Global Health: Who Runs the World and Why?* She is also the Vice Chair of the Clinton Foundation, where she works on many initiatives, including those that help empower the next generation of leaders. She lives in New York City with her husband, Marc, their children and their dog, Soren.

You can follow Chelsea Clinton on Twitter
@ChelseaClinton
or on Facebook at
facebook.com/chelseaclinton

ALEXANDRA BOIGER has illustrated nearly twenty picture books, including the She Persisted books by Chelsea Clinton; the popular Tallulah series by Marilyn Singer; and the Max and Marla books, which she also wrote. Originally from Munich, Germany, she now lives outside of San Francisco, California, with her husband, Andrea, daughter, Vanessa, and two cats, Luiso and Winter.

You can visit Alexandra Boiger online at
alexandraboiger.com
or follow her on Instagram
@alexandra_boiger

Read about more inspiring women in the

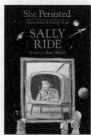

She Persisted series!

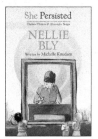
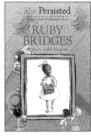

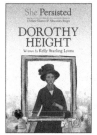
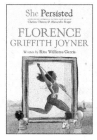

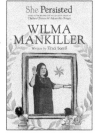

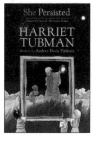
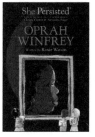
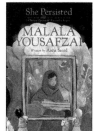